TWO LITTLE GOLFERS
BEING POSITIVE

Written by Jenn Holt

Illustration by Harry Aveira

Two Little Golfers
Being Positive
All Rights Reserved.
Copyright © 2019 Jenn Holt
v1.0

This is a work of fiction. The events and characters described herein are imaginary and are not intended to refer to specific places or living persons. The opinions expressed in this manuscript are solely the opinions of the author and do not represent the opinions or thoughts of the publisher. The author has represented and warranted full ownership and/or legal right to publish all the materials in this book.

This book may not be reproduced, transmitted, or stored in whole or in part by any means, including graphic, electronic, or mechanical without the express written consent of the publisher except in the case of brief quotations embodied in critical articles and reviews.

Outskirts Press, Inc.
http://www.outskirtspress.com

Paperback ISBN: 978-1-9772-0126-3
Hardback ISBN: 978-1-9772-0128-7

Illustrations © 2019 Harry Aveira. All rights reserved - used with permission.

Outskirts Press and the "OP" logo are trademarks belonging to Outskirts Press, Inc.

PRINTED IN THE UNITED STATES OF AMERICA

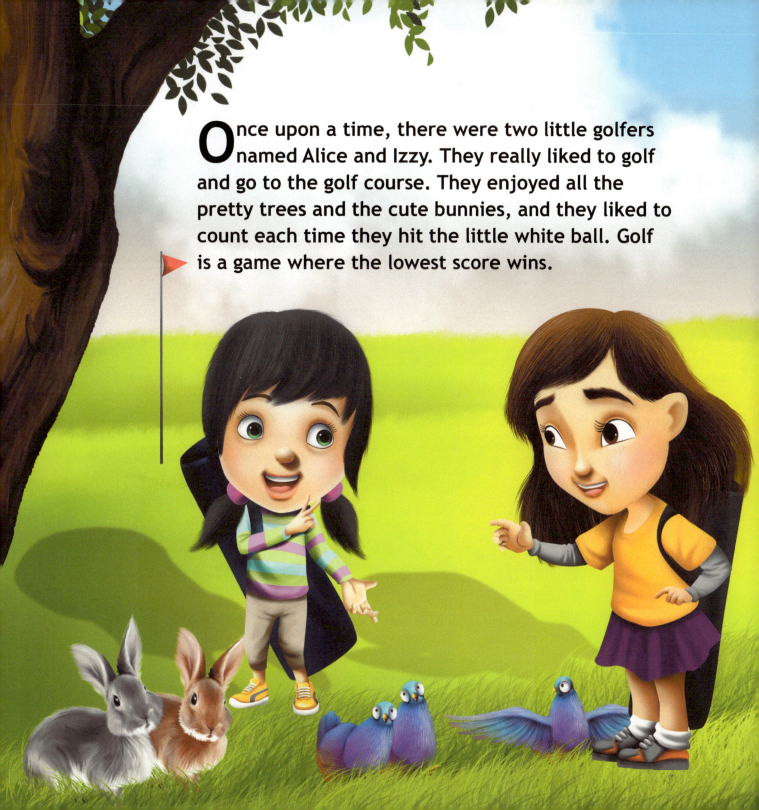

Once upon a time, there were two little golfers named Alice and Izzy. They really liked to golf and go to the golf course. They enjoyed all the pretty trees and the cute bunnies, and they liked to count each time they hit the little white ball. Golf is a game where the lowest score wins.

One day, Izzy and Alice went to play nine holes with their golf coach, Jenn.

"It's a beautiful day!" Coach Jenn remarked. "Let's have some fun!"

On the first hole, a par four, Izzy hit a spectacular drive down the middle of the fairway. She was sooooo happy and all smiles.

Next Alice stepped up and swung at the ball. But guess what? She missed it! Poor Alice was sooooo embarrassed. She pouted and said, "I'm not good at golf!"

Coach Jenn said, "Alice, I only want to hear positive words. Take a deep breath and try again."

So Alice tried to hit the ball, and guess what? She hit it super far, even past Izzy's ball!

Izzy was happy for Alice and said, "Wow, awesome shot! Way to go!" Izzy always seemed to be positive.

Not Alice. She continued to pout and thought, I missed the first ball so now I'm hitting number three. She was not happy. Alice kept telling herself, "Golf is so hard."

It was Izzy's turn to hit her second shot. She hit a really bad one that only went two feet. That's called a "chunk" in golf. But Izzy didn't mind. Instead she laughed a little bit and said, "Oh well, I bet the next shot will be amazing."

Coach Jenn was so proud of Izzy's positive attitude. It was still Izzy's turn because her ball was farthest from the hole. *Whack!* Izzy swung, and the ball went sailing onto the green! "Amazing, just like I thought," she said.

Now it was Alice's turn again. Sadly, she said to herself, "This ball probably won't go on the green. I'm not as good as Izzy." And guess what? She hit the ball softly, and it rolled and rolled but did not get to the green. Alice slumped her shoulders and said, "Golf is hard."

Coach Jenn heard her and said, "Alice, everything is hard when you first try it. That's why you need to practice a lot to make it easier."

Izzy added, "Yeah, it was hard for me, too, when I started to golf. I just try to stay happy no matter what kind of shot I make, and now golf is a lot more fun."

"Yes," Coach Jenn said. "Be positive *always*."

Because Alice's ball was farther away from the hole, it was her turn. "Remember, Alice," said Coach Jenn, "no matter how you hit this shot, be happy and positive."

"Okay," Alice said slowly, not sure she could do that. She stood over her chip shot and said to herself, "No matter what happens, I will smile after this shot." And guess what? Alice hit a beautiful chip, fifteen feet from the hole.

"Wow! Great shot, Alice!" said Coach Jenn and Izzy.

Alice smiled and said, "Thank you." She was so happy because of her good shot.

Now it was Izzy's turn to hit her forty-foot putt. That's a long way!

"Tick-tock," Izzy said as the ball started to roll, but it stopped ten feet from the hole. "That was not a very good putt, but that's okay. I can still get my next shot in."

Again Alice's ball was the farthest away, so she had to putt. What if I miss it? thought Alice.

Right then Coach Jenn reminded her, "Remember, Alice, no matter what happens to this putt, I want to see a smile on your face afterward."

"Okay," said Alice, not really sure she could do that. "Tick-tock," she said and putted. Whoosh! She hit the ball way past the hole, about fifteen feet. Oh no! Alice let out a big groan. "Ugh, that was--"

Suddenly Coach Jenn interrupted her. "What? Remember, you must smile; that's all, Alice. No complaining."

So Alice reluctantly smiled.

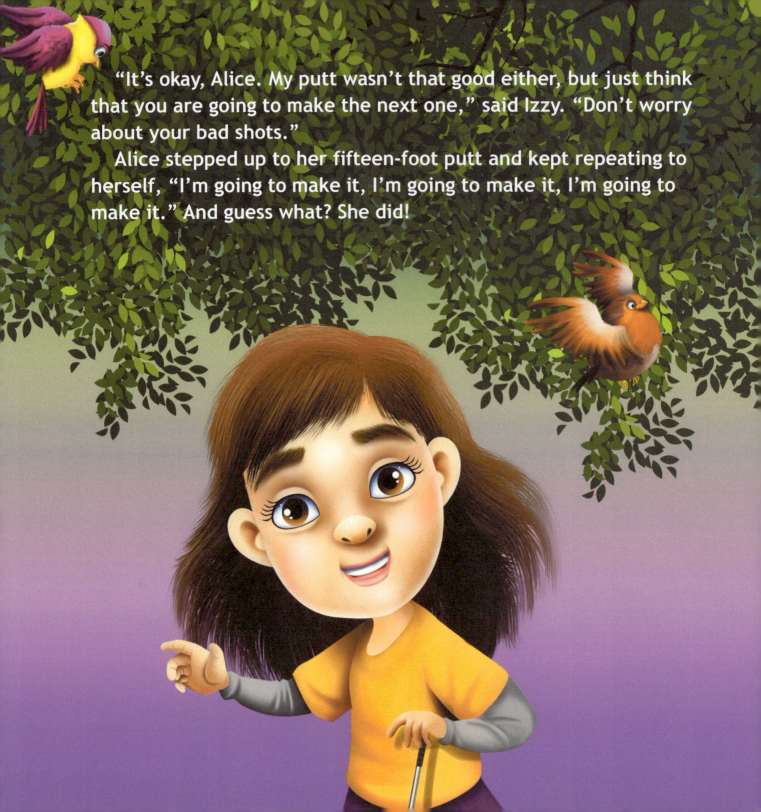

"It's okay, Alice. My putt wasn't that good either, but just think that you are going to make the next one," said Izzy. "Don't worry about your bad shots."

Alice stepped up to her fifteen-foot putt and kept repeating to herself, "I'm going to make it, I'm going to make it, I'm going to make it." And guess what? She did!

"Great putt, Alice!" said Coach Jenn.

"Nice putt!" said Izzy.

"You must have been thinking positive thoughts before you hit that ball," Coach Jenn said.

"Yes. I kept telling myself, 'I can make that putt,'" Alice said.

"See? Life is happier when you're positive," said Coach Jenn.

They were almost done with the first hole, but first Izzy had to finish her putting. "Tick-tock," Izzy said as she hit the ball. Oh no! She hit it too softly. "That's okay. I better practice my putting more," Izzy said and laughed. After tapping in for a three putt, she was still smiling.

Alice was amazed. I want to be positive just like her, she thought.

"I'm really proud of you two for learning how to become positive and stay positive, even when you hit bad shots," Coach Jenn told them.

And with that said, they happily walked to hole number two and had a great afternoon on the golf course.

Can you name some negative thoughts and then some positive thoughts and write them down on this page?

CPSIA information can be obtained
at www.ICGtesting.com
Printed in the USA
LVHW070513211118
597619LV00002BA/26/P